WPPSI™-IV Test

Processing Speed

Practice Book

Improve

Processing Speed:

- Bug Search
- Animal Coding
- Cancellation

Zoe Hampton

Published by Perfect Consulting B.V.

Other IQ books by the author
https://prfc.nl/go/amznbooks

SCAN ME

   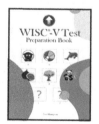

Our Mobile Applications for IQ Training

https://prfc.nl/go/allapps

Follow us on social media

Web site: https://prfc.nl/go/pc

Facebook: https://prfc.nl/go/fbpc

Instagram: https://prfc.nl/go/inpc

LinkedIn: https://prfc.nl/go/lipc

YouTube: https://prfc.nl/go/ytpc

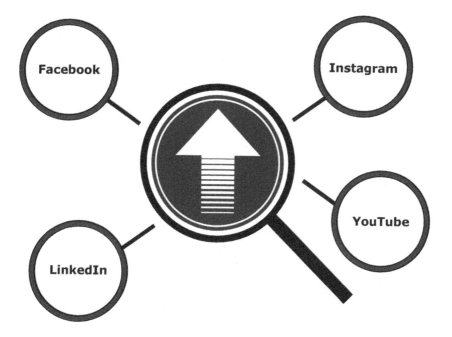

Introduction

WPPSI™-IV Test
Processing Speed Practice Book

The Weschler Preschool and Primary Scale of Intelligence™/WPPSI™ is used to test intelligence in children aged 2 years 6 months to 7 years 7 months. It consists of 15 subtests. The WPPSI™ assesses skills and talents rather than grade-level information. The test examines cognitive abilities, problem-solving, decision-making, and thinking processes. The WPPSI™ score is summarized into five primary areas: Verbal Comprehension Index (VCI), Visual Spatial Index (VSI), Fluid Reasoning Index (FRI), Working Memory Index (WMI) and Processing Speed Index (PSI).

This practice book contains exercises for the Processing Speed. The Processing Speed Index (PSI) measures a student's ability to complete scanning and sequencing tasks quickly and correctly, as well as discriminate between simple visual information provided.

About this book

The WPPSI™-IV Test Processing Speed Practice book shows children about the format, topics, and difficulty level of WPPSI™ test questions. These exercises will assist your child to improve his/her WPPSI™-IV test-taking skills. The book contains exercises from the following subtests:
- Bug Search
- Animal Coding
- Cancellation

Table of Contents

Bug Search

The Bug Search subtest is a child-friendly version of Symbol Search. Symbol Search is a timed Processing Speed test. This subtest assesses how quickly your child completes a timed test, or how fast they process information. The activity requires visual-spatial reasoning, thinking, and memory skills.

This test shows rows of animals. The child must concentrate and remember the first animal at the start of each row, then look for the same animal among the other animals in the row.

Instructions:

1. Show the child the first row of animals and tell him to remember the first animal and find the same animal among the remaining animals in the row.

2. The test is timed. Within 120 seconds, the child must mark each repeating animal in the set.

Bug Search

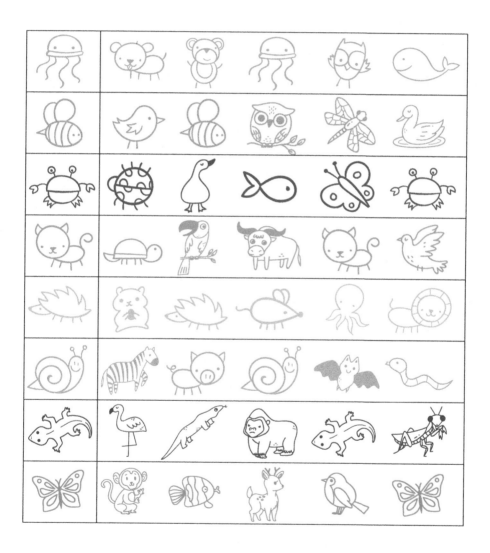

Bug Search

3 Bug Search

4 Bug Search

12

Animal Coding

Animal Coding is a form of Coding that pairs known and appealing animals with simple shapes. Animal Coding is a timed paired-associates subtest in which the child marks shapes that match to animals. This subtest assesses how quickly your child completes a timed test, or how fast they process information. The activity requires visual-spatial reasoning, thinking, and memory skills.

This test shows three colored boxes, each with a picture and a figure under it. The child must concentrate and remember which figure corresponds which picture.

Instructions:

1. Show the child the three colored boxes that begin each set. Explain that each picture has a figure that corresponds to the picture above it. Work together to identify and mark (X) the matching figures in the first set.
2. The test is timed. Within 120 seconds, the child must mark each corresponding figure in the set.

Animal Coding

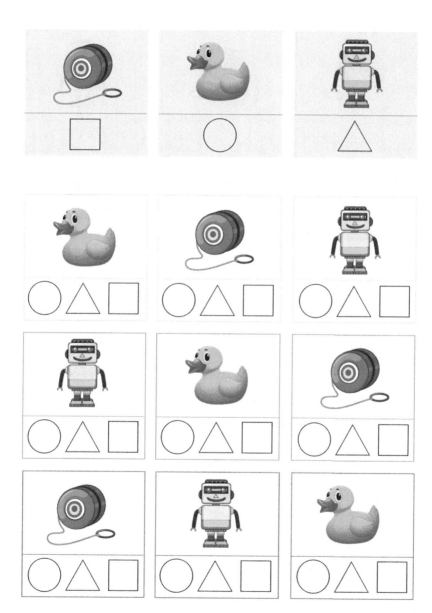

1 Animal Coding

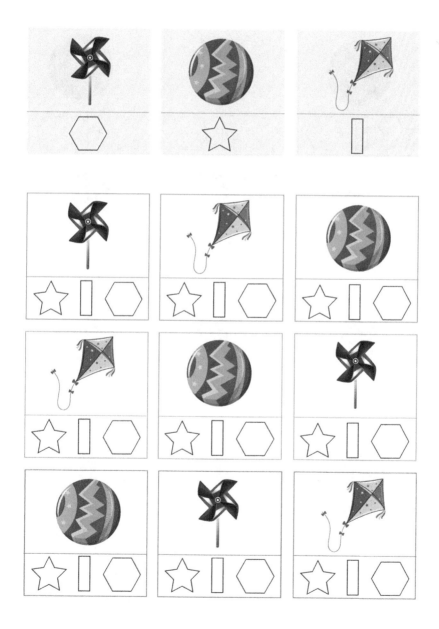

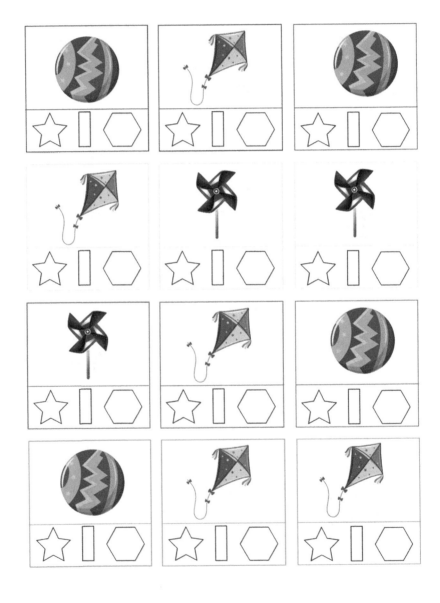

Animal Coding

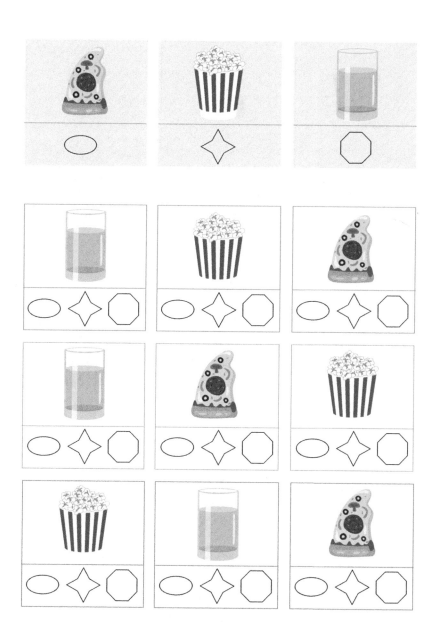

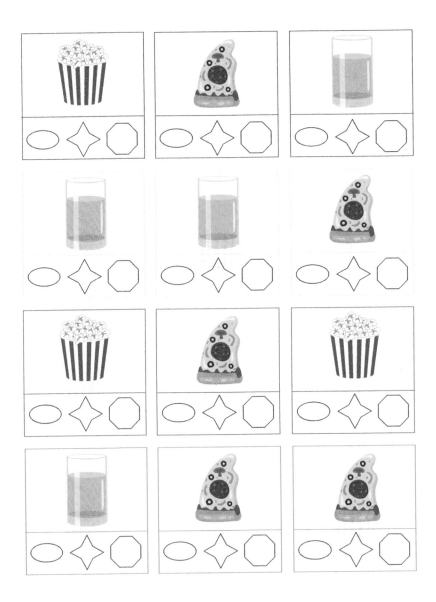

4 Animal Coding

4 Animal Coding

5 Animal Coding

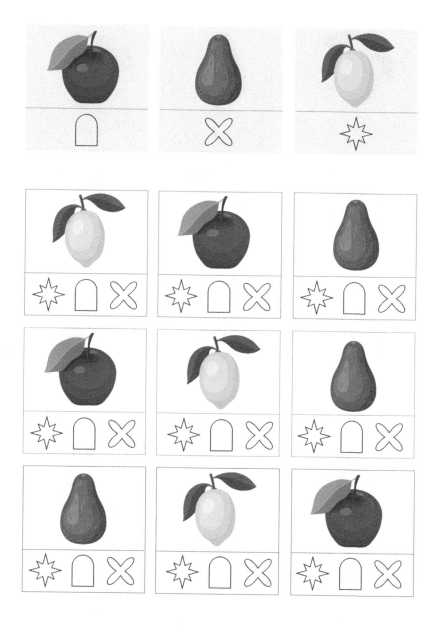

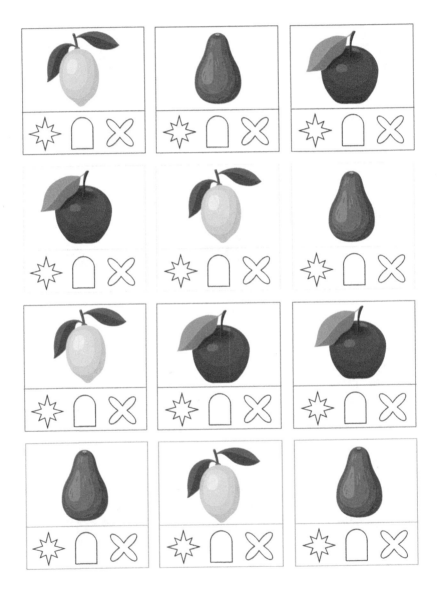

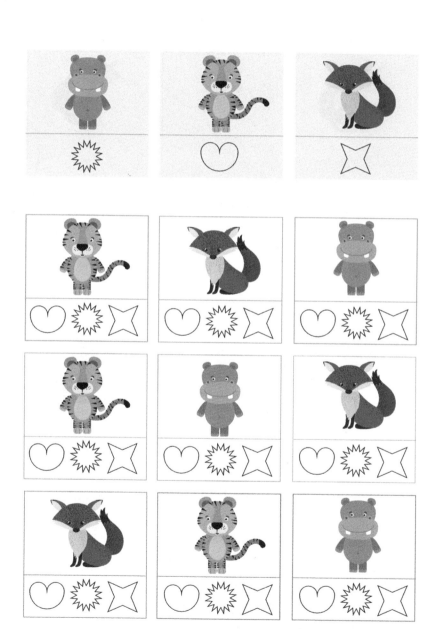

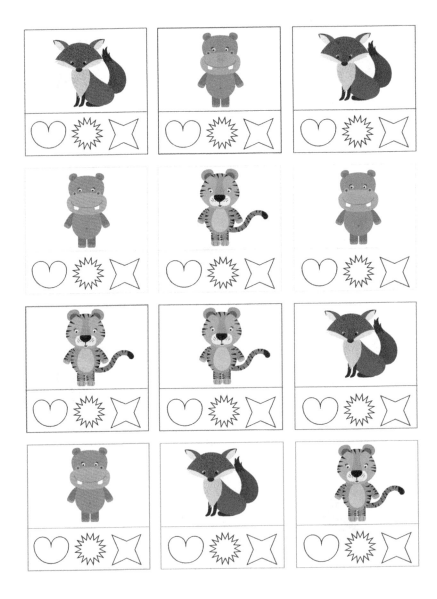

28

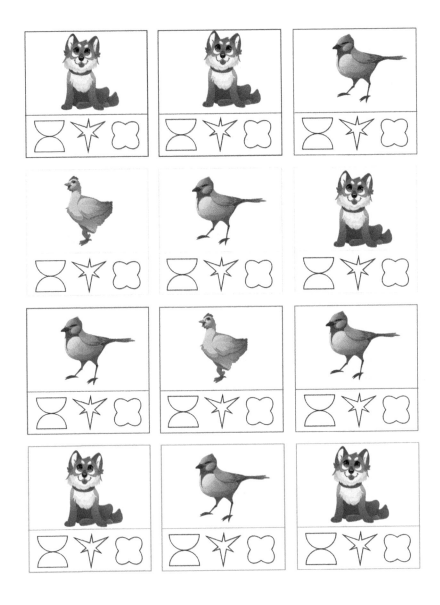

Animal Coding

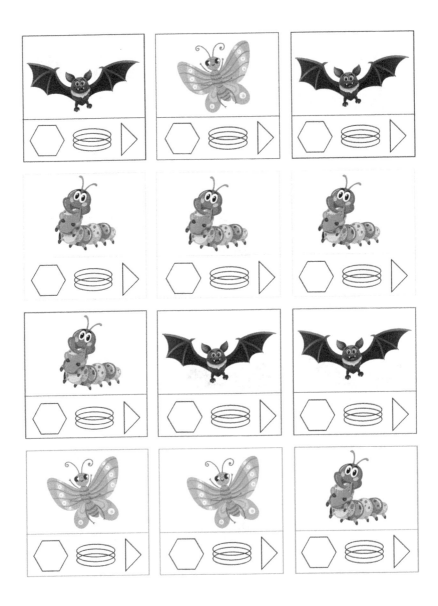

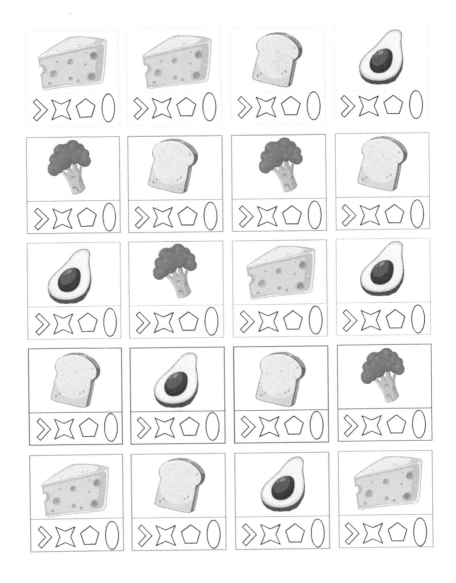

Animal Coding

Animal Coding

12

Animal Coding

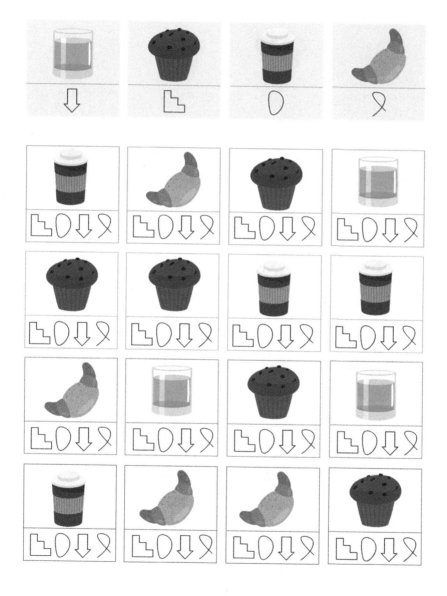

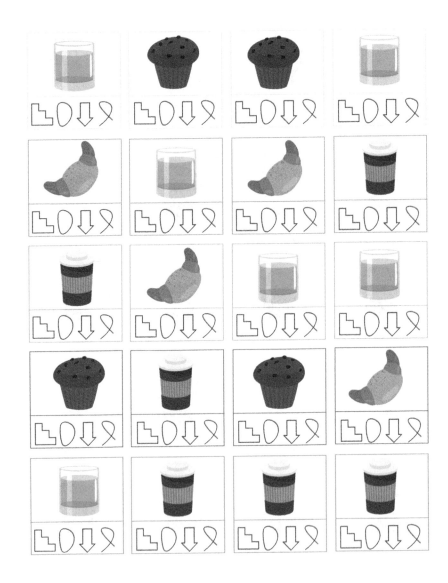

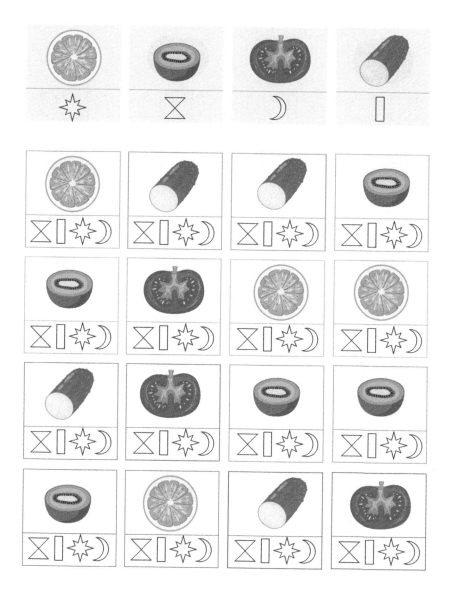

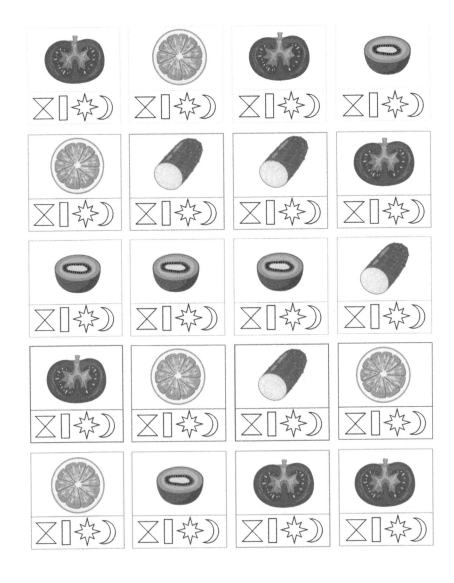

Animal Coding

16 Animal Coding

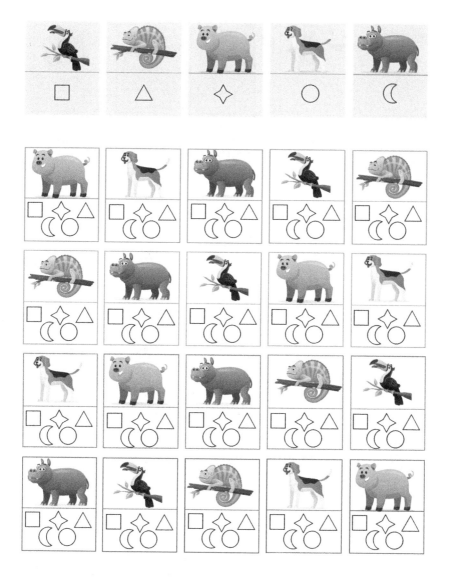

45

16 Animal Coding

46

Animal Coding

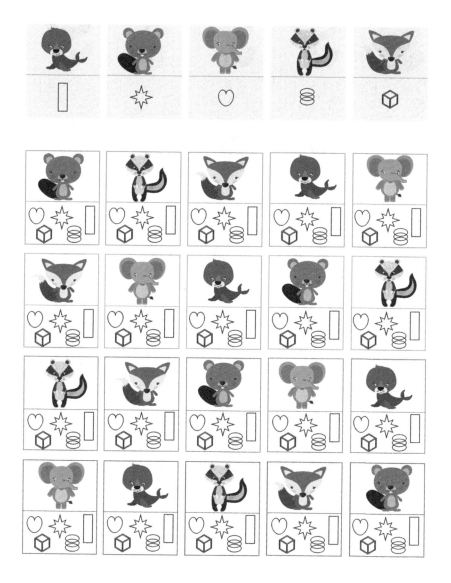

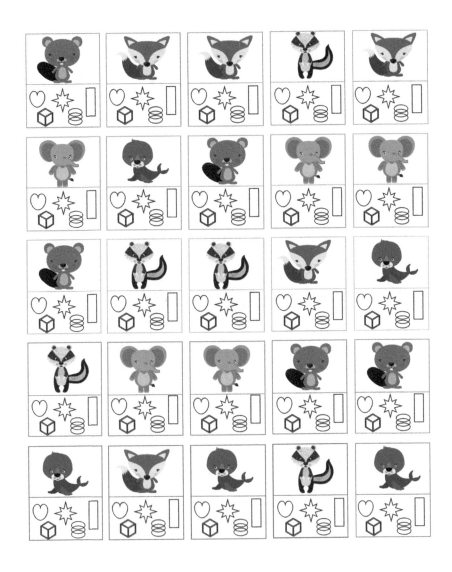

Animal Coding

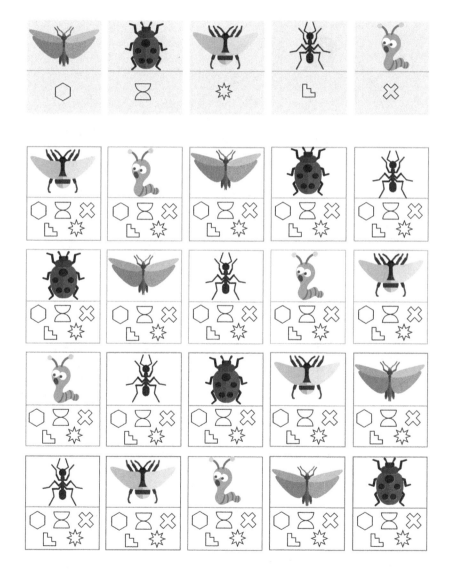

Animal Coding

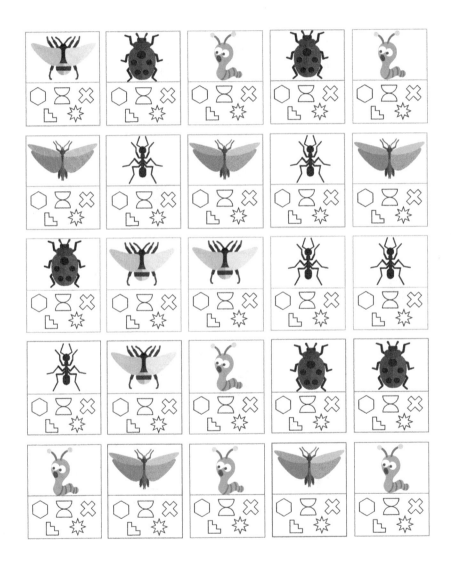

19 Animal Coding

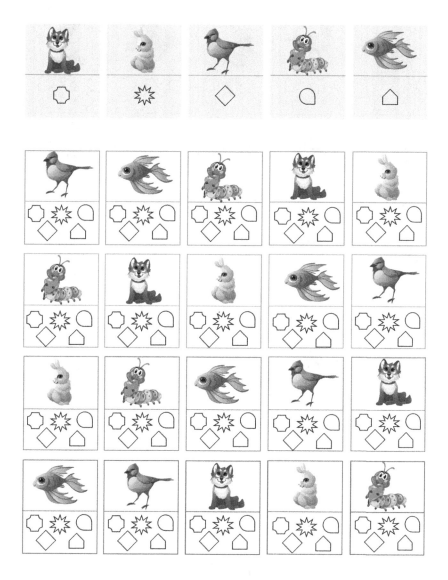

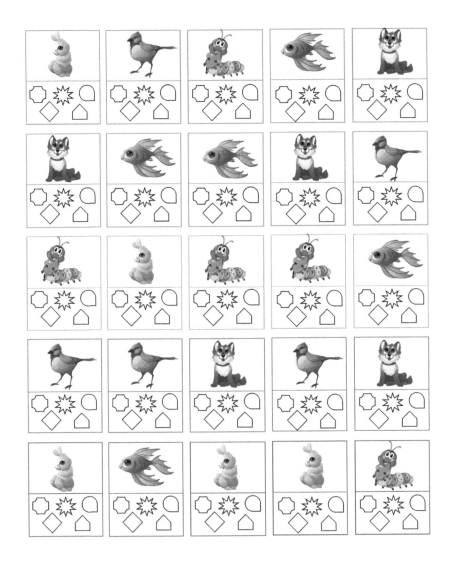

Cancellation

Cancellation is a processing speed test in which a child analyses two arrangements of items (one random and one structured) and selects the target objects. This subtest assesses how quickly your child completes a timed test, or how fast they process information. The activity requires visual-spatial reasoning, thinking, and memory skills.
The test shows target items in a single row. There are many objects below them, and the child must only mark those that are the same as those specified in the first row.

Instructions:
1. Show the child the first row, which contains the target objects, then show the items below them and explain that the child must find and mark (X) the items that match the top row.
2. The test is timed. Within 45 seconds, the child must mark each corresponding items in the set.

1 Cancellation

4 Cancellation

5 Cancellation

6 Cancellation

7 Cancellation

8 Cancellation

9　Cancellation

10 Cancellation

ANSWERS

Bug Search
(answers)

1

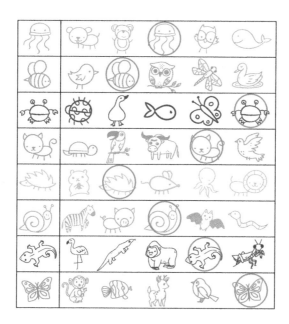

2

Bug Search
(answers)

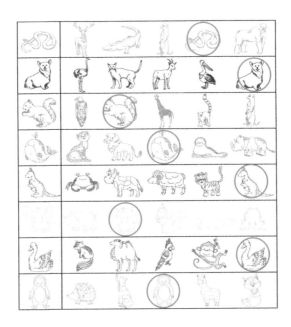

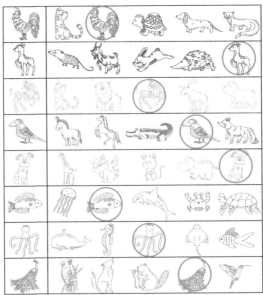

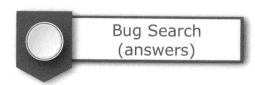

Bug Search
(answers)

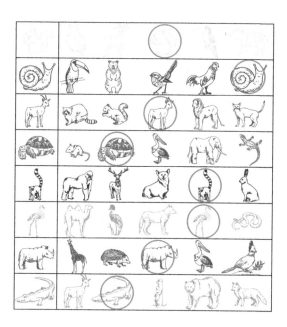

Animal Coding
(answers)

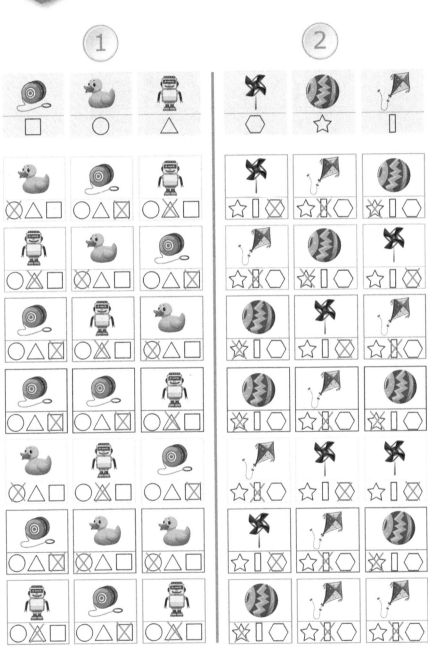

Animal Coding (answers)

③

④

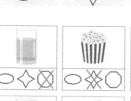 

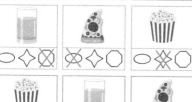 

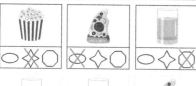 

Animal Coding
(answers)

⑤ ⑥

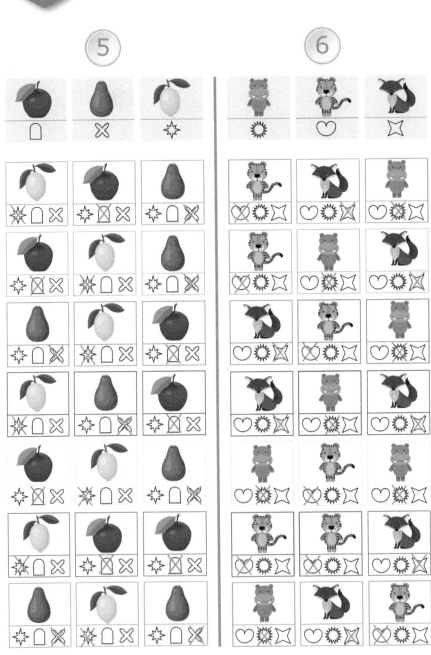

Animal Coding
(answers)

⑦

⑧

73

Animal Coding
(answers)

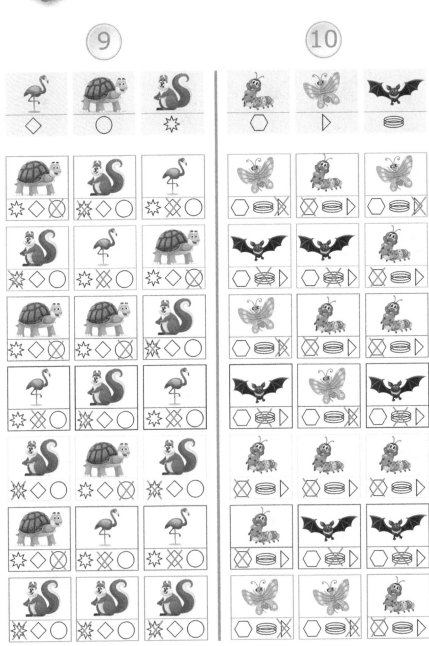

11

12

15

16

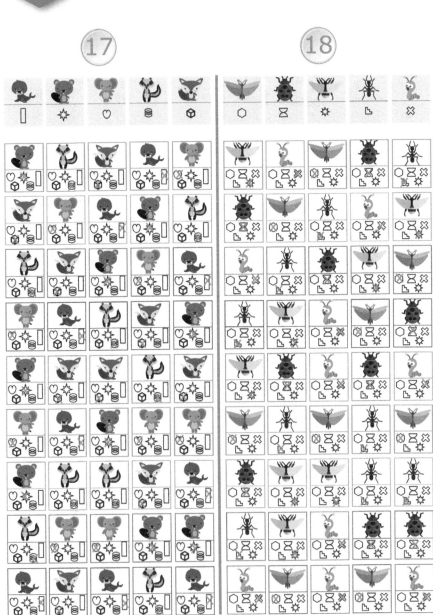

Animal Coding (answers)

19   20

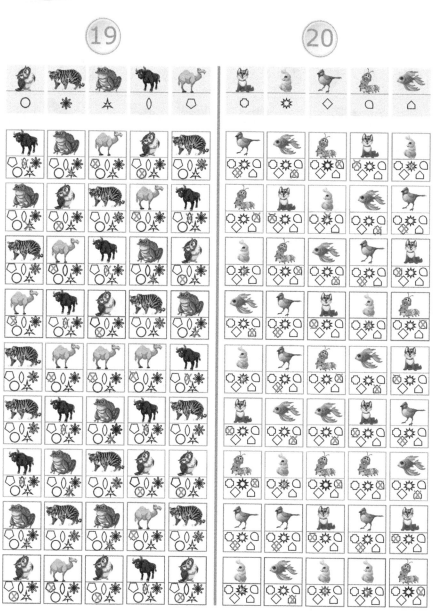

79

Cancellation
(answers)

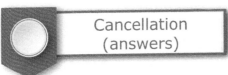

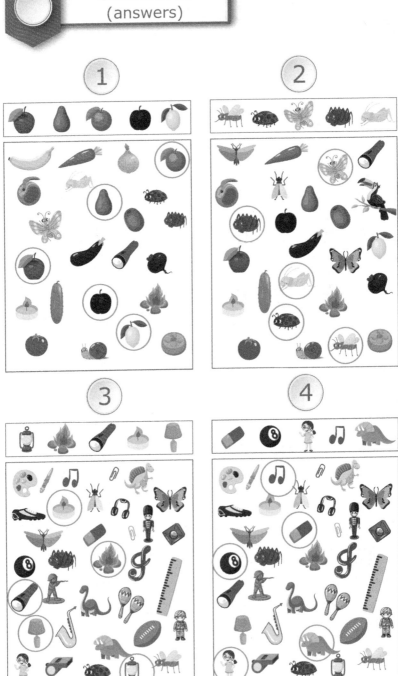

Cancellation
(answers)

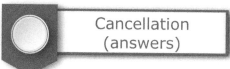

Cancellation
(answers)

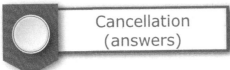

Thank you for your purchase!
I hope you enjoyed this book!

Please consider leaving a review!
https://prfc.nl/go/abreview

Made in the USA
Coppell, TX
02 December 2024

41540376R00046